CONTENTS

Written by Philippa Forrester

Collins

THE LONGEST RIVER IN THE WORLD

The Nile is the longest river in the world. For around 6,650 kilometres this mighty African river flows north through 11 different countries, jungles, mountains and even the Sahara desert.

The Nile starts with two smaller rivers – the White Nile and the Blue Nile. The White Nile flows from mountains in Burundi and Rwanda into Lake Victoria, which is in both Tanzania and Uganda. The river enters the lake in Tanzania and leaves it in Uganda. This is thought of as the source of the Nile.

The Blue Nile starts at Lake Tana in Ethiopia, and flows through deep gorges and a huge canyon to Sudan.
In the rainy season, the Blue Nile floods, sweeping up fertile soil from the Ethiopian Highlands and carrying it along the river as **silt**.

In Khartoum, Sudan, the White and Blue Nile combine to form the Nile, which flows through the harsh deserts of Egypt before finally ending at the Mediterranean Sea.

Cairo
Nile
EGYPT
Lake Nasser
Red Sea
Khartoum
SUDAN
White Nile
Blue Nile
Lake Tana
ETHIOPIA
SOUTH SUDAN
UGANDA
RWANDA
BURUNDI
Lake Victoria
TANZANIA

The Nile's annual floods, bringing water and nutrient-rich silt to the desert lands, were the reason humans were able to settle here, becoming farmers around 7,000 years ago.

Two kingdoms then emerged in ancient Egypt, one along the lower and one along the upper Nile, but by 3,100 BCE the first Egyptian **pharaoh**, Narmer, made them one kingdom. Unfortunately, the Nile would also be the cause of his death, as he was said to have been killed by a hippopotamus.

Ancient Egypt was one of the most advanced civilisations in the world at that time, and we have been left with a history that is rich in culture, **hieroglyphs**, and religion stretching back thousands of years.

Throughout history, the mighty Nile river has been a vital source of water and food, and it's still a place where humans thrive today.

Imagine what it might be like to take a journey along the Nile ...

Did you know?

Some people think that the name "Nile" comes from Ancient Greek and Latin words, *Neilos* (meaning river valley) and *Nilus* (meaning river).

Mediterranean Sea

Alexandria

NILE DELTA

Cairo

Nile

NILE VALLEY

EGYPT

Red Sea

Luxor

Esna

Edfu

Kom Ombo

Elephantine Island

Aswan Dam

Lake Nasser

1 LAKE NASSER AND THE ASWAN DAM

Our journey through Egypt begins on top of the Aswan Dam. When it was finished, in 1970, it was the tallest dam in the world at 111 metres. It was named after the nearby city of Aswan and built to protect towns along the river from flooding, to create electricity and to provide ways to regulate the water for farmers.

The dam has changed the Nile and life around it in many ways, but especially by creating one of the largest man-made lakes in the world.

Nile
Aswan Dam
Lake
Nasser

Lake Nasser is vast. Rocky islands poke up from the water's surface and temples sit on its banks. Nile crocodiles, jackals, desert foxes and even hyenas live in and around the water. On the shores, herdsmen graze sheep and camels.

When the Aswan Dam was finished, blocking the Nile, it took six years for the water to fill the lake. A lake created in this way is called a reservoir. Slowly, the Nile's water flooded 5,000 square kilometres of the Nile Valley, and the lake is now 90 metres deep.

Not everyone welcomed this new reservoir to Egypt. This huge valley was home to around 100,000 people, who all had to move from an area formerly known as Nubia and resettle to new homes.

The rising waters also threatened many ancient Egyptian temples. A huge international campaign, the UNESCO Nubian salvage campaign, saved many of them. At a cost of over 80 million dollars, the temples were carefully cut into pieces, moved and reassembled on the banks away from the water.

THE NUBIAN MONUMENTS

The Temple of Kalabsha

The Temple of Kalabsha was saved when the Aswan Dam was constructed. Built during the time of the early Romans in 30 BCE, it was a tribute to a sun god, with many precious inscriptions carved into the walls. It took two years to move the temple, which now sits on its own island in the lake.

carvings in Beit al-Wali Temple, Kalabsha

The Abu Simbel temples

The Abu Simbel temples were built by the famous Pharaoh Rameses II about 3,000 years ago, to remind everyone of his power and mark the southern border of ancient Egypt with Nubia. The figure of Rameses II sits with his wife, Nefertiti, and their children.

Centuries in the desert almost buried the temples under sand. They were rediscovered in the early 1800s and dug out, then years later rescued again from the lake and moved to higher ground.

In this engraving from the temple, Rameses makes an offering to the god Horus, who was protector of pharaohs.

TOURISM

Today, Lake Nasser is a thriving tourist centre, bringing much-needed money to a desert area with few natural resources.

Cruise ships carry hundreds of visitors around the lake every day to visit the rescued Nubian monuments.

Many tourists come for fishing. Lake Nasser is famous for huge Nile perch, which share the waters with 18 species of tigerfish, tilapia, giant catfish, moonfish and many others.

The Nile perch

The Nile perch has lived on the Nile for millions of years and is the biggest fish predator here. A Nile perch can weigh over 200 kilograms (more than a giant panda) and be over two metres tall, (taller than a very tall person).

Ancient Egyptian gods

Neith was the goddess of creation, war and hunting, and was known as "the great mother". Her story begins before Earth was created. In the form of a Nile perch, she lit up her eyes, bringing light to the universe.

WHY DID EGYPT NEED TO BUILD THE ASWAN DAM?

The Aswan Dam was created for three main reasons.

1. To create hydroelectric power

Hydroelectric power is created when falling water moves turbines. The dam forces water from Lake Nasser through turbines which spin a generator to create electricity.

This type of environmentally-friendly energy, known as “renewable” or “green” energy, doesn’t burn any fossil fuels. Instead, it just relies on a flow of water.

The Aswan Dam has 12 electricity generators. At first it created electricity for villages which had never had it before. It supplied enough for almost half of Egypt’s electricity needs, but modern-day Egypt demands more and more electricity.

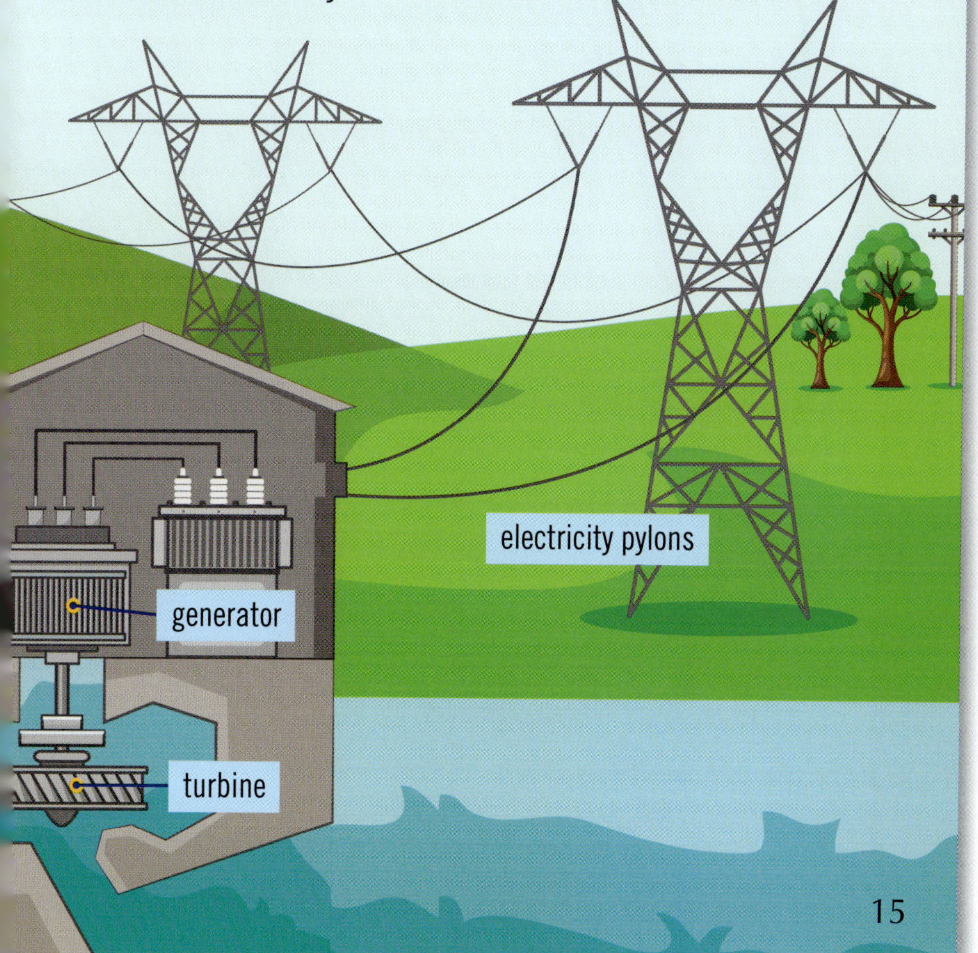

2. To regulate flooding

In years of heavy rainfall, the Nile would flood, and in years of drought there wouldn't be enough water to grow crops. Water levels can now be regulated by the dam so that water is always available.

Since the dam was built, Egypt has experienced two droughts which would have meant a severe water shortage if the dam and lake hadn't existed.

Ancient Egyptian gods

Hapy was thought to control the flooding of the Nile river and all life that depended on it. He was worshipped as a symbol of fertility and good food, and often had flowers or plants growing from his head.

3. To increase crop production

It hardly ever rains in Egypt, so Egyptian farmers depend entirely on the Nile for water. Because the dam now controls the flow, a regular, year-round water supply can be provided. Roughly 300 square kilometres of desert land has been reclaimed for farmers who can now rely on growing one or even two crops a year.

watering crops

THE FEROCIOUS NILE CROCODILE

Nile crocodiles are some of the largest and most fearsome predators in the world and live throughout Africa. They are dangerous and thought to kill 200 people a year.

Nile crocodiles live in the parts of Africa that are coloured green here.

Nile crocodiles do have a tender side; just before their eggs hatch, the baby crocodiles inside make a high-pitched noise, making their mother dig up the nest. She picks up the tiny hatchlings and carries them to the water. The mother guards her baby crocodiles for up to two years.

Although ancient Egyptians worshipped them, between the 1940s and 1960s they became endangered, as more and more humans invaded their territory and hunted them for their leathery skin. They are now protected by law, but they are still under threat from illegal poachers.

Crocodiles no longer live on the Nile river in Egypt. The riverbanks are busy with humans, and the Aswan Dam made water levels in the river drop, so the river is no longer a good habitat for them. Many crocodiles moved from the river to Lake Nasser, where they flourished.

2 THE NILE VALLEY

Just north of the Aswan Dam lies a rough, shallow, rocky area of water called a **rapid**, which is impossible to sail across. Through history, this has been seen as a useful border, protecting ancient Egypt from the world beyond and meaning no one could sail all the way along the Nile.

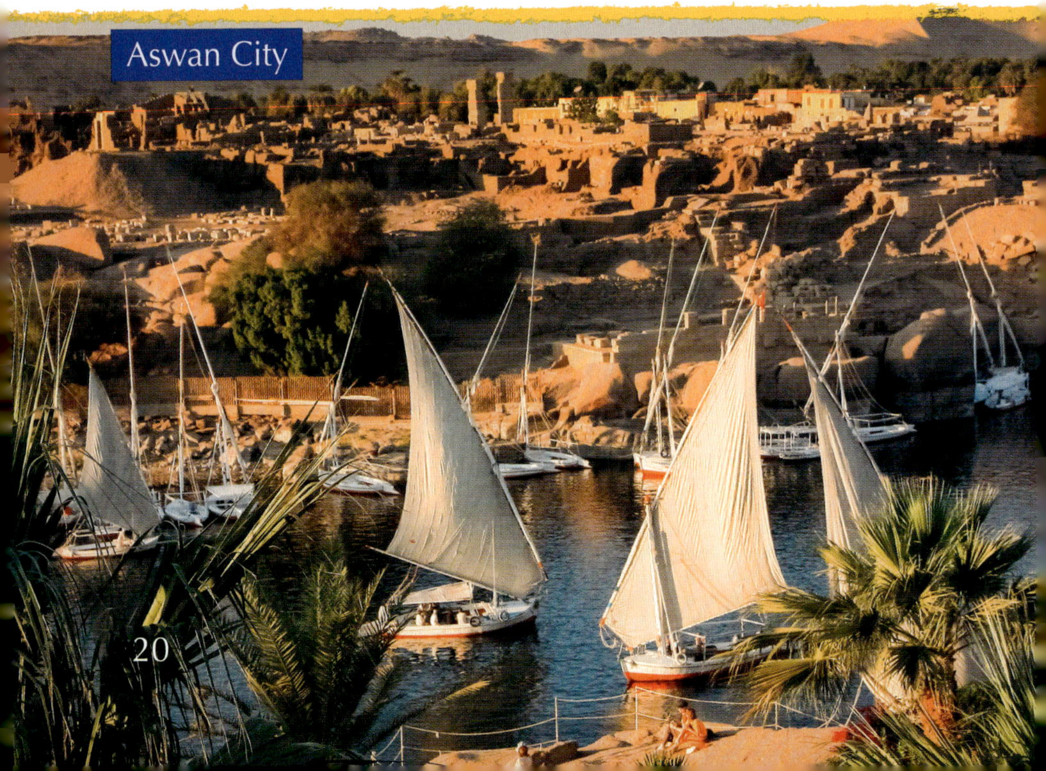

Aswan City

Leaving the roaring waters of the Aswan Dam behind, we continue north along the Nile Valley. In ancient times, this area was known as Upper Egypt.

The city of Aswan, known as Swenet in ancient Egypt, lies on the East Bank. Its ancient name came from the hard granite rock that was mined here.

The rock was used to build many ancient statues and temples. Many of these can still be seen up and down the Nile today, but some were buried over time and forgotten about. One exciting find in the late 19th century was the Unfinished Obelisk, still lying in the ground where it was being carved. At 42 metres long and over 1,200 tonnes, this gigantic piece of granite, if it had been finished, would have been the biggest obelisk ever erected.

In high cliffs opposite Aswan are the Tombs of the Nobles. These tombs are around 3,000 years old and contain colourful wall images showing the everyday life and adventures of the nobles – people who supported the pharaohs.

the Tombs of the Nobles

In the middle of the river lies Elephantine Island. Some people say it was named after large, submerged rocks in the water which look like elephants.

Elephantine Island

This small island was an important trading place in ancient Egypt. Traders from other parts of Africa would bring ivory here to sell. As ivory comes from elephant tusks, perhaps that might have been another reason for its unusual name. Today the ivory trade is banned in Africa to protect elephants.

The ancient Egyptians thought Elephantine was home to the god Khnum, who they believed ruled over all water, including the Nile. The ruins of the temple to Khnum can still be seen today.

The island is now a protected World Heritage site and is looked after so we can enjoy it for many more centuries to come.

Did you know?

Nilometers on Elephantine Island

Ancient Egyptians were so aware of the importance of the Nile's water level that they measured it regularly, especially the height of the annual floods. By cutting graduated scales in rocks or walls along the riverbank, they were able to use them like a measuring stick and keep accurate records.

In those days, the reason for the rise and fall of the Nile was a mystery. Today we know that it's caused by heavy rainfall far away in Ethiopia and in the desert to the east.

From Aswan, it's possible to take a boat all the way down the rest of the Nile as it flows through narrow, green valleys.

This area has very little rainfall, so without the river's water it would just be desert. When it floods, the river carries black, nutrient-rich silt. As the flood waters drain away, this rich silt is left behind and feeds the soil. Throughout history, this great combination of fertile soil and water has helped plants grow well on this narrow band of land beside the river, which has helped humans to survive.

Palm trees are dotted along the shores of the river. Sheep and water buffalo graze on the banks and **sand spits**, and families gather water each day. Fishermen stand in simple rowing boats to cast their nets.

Settlements have grown alongside the river. Low buildings with small windows cling to the shores where cattle and goats drink.

In some places, the sandstone banks are steep, rising like cliffs on either side of the river. In ancient Egypt, sandstone blocks were cut from these rocks and floated downstream to help build cities like Luxor.

The river also passes through larger towns with roads and even industrial areas.

IRRIGATION

For thousands of years, water from the Nile has allowed life in the desert to flourish. Humans have made the most of it by using irrigation. Irrigation involves using canals, or small trenches, to spread water around crops like wheat, barley, cotton and beans. This was the key to growing food in this dry, arid place. It's thought that irrigation began as long ago as 3100 BCE. An engraving from that time even seems to show the Scorpion king cutting open an irrigation channel.

This engraving shows the King himself using a hoe to open a water canal.

Ancient Egyptian gods

Isis was the goddess of protection, motherhood and magic. The ancient Egyptians thought the Nile floods were created by the tears she cried for her dead husband Osiris.

SHADUF

Farmers in ancient Egypt used a "crane" called a *shaduf* to move water from the river to their systems of canals and ditches.

Later, waterwheels and other methods did the job. Using the Nile's water to grow food and support the population is what enabled the ancient Egyptians to become one of the most long-lasting and powerful civilisations in history.

The Egyptian year was even divided into three seasons according to the cycles of the Nile:

1. Akhet – the summer flooding season
2. Peret – the growing season
3. Shemu – harvesting season

Today, the Aswan Dam provides a way to control the water, and now Egyptians can rely on regular water.

KOM OMBO

Continuing our journey along the Nile towards the sea, we sail through an area famous for its sugar cane plantations. We turn a bend in the river and see the temple of Kom Ombo. Inside, ancient carvings and hieroglyphs tell stories of rituals and medical practices, including pictures of the tools needed for medical surgery.

This is an unusual double temple, half dedicated to the god Horus and half to the god Sobek, with sanctuaries and inscriptions for each one. Kom Ombo has its own crocodile pool where sacred crocodiles were kept, and ancient Egyptians would even feed them human food.

Ancient Egyptian gods

Sobek was depicted with the head of a crocodile and the body of a human, or sometimes fully as a crocodile. People lived in fear and respect of crocodiles on the Nile, so they worshipped Sobek to keep them safe, for his association with the river and because some believed he controlled the floods that they relied on to grow their crops.

Crocodiles were so respected in ancient Egypt that when one died, it was **mummified** and buried like a pharaoh. Some were given ivory or gold teeth or eyes.

Many mummified crocodiles have been found at Kom Ombo as offerings to Sobek, and are displayed in a crocodile museum next to the temple.

a mummified crocodile

EDFU

The next main temple along the river is set in the crowded city of Edfu.

This temple is dedicated to the falcon-headed god of the sky, Horus. It is one of the best preserved of all. It took around 180 years to build, between 237 BCE and 57 BCE, and was one of the largest temples for one of the most important gods. A grand entrance, the pylon, has huge, engraved pillars at either side.

A series of rooms, halls and chapels follow with many statues of Horus. Egyptians celebrated Horus and their pharaoh with annual festivals, sometimes lasting for two weeks. Inscriptions and pictures on the walls tell us about Horus, and give us lots of information about the ancient Egyptian way of life.

Ancient Egyptian gods

Horus was the god of war and hunting. He was believed to be part-man and part-falcon, and was often depicted with a falcon's head.

ESNA

After passing between green banks of farmland with desert rising behind them, the busy city of Esna is our next stop. With two major roads connecting Egypt with Europe, as well as the Nile, Esna became a famous trade centre for traders from the Red Sea and all over Africa. In the 17th and 18th centuries, camels, spices and even elephants were traded here. Today, the ancient markets still bustle with cotton and spices and modern goods, bought by tourists.

The temple at Esna was dedicated to the god Khnum.

Ancient Egyptian gods

Khnum, with a ram or sheep's head, was thought to be guardian of the Nile's source and its flooding. He was also a craftsman who could use the river's clay to create humans.

LUXOR AND THE VALLEY OF THE KINGS

About 50 kilometres north of Esna, Luxor is a huge, modern city where the East Bank is crowded by modern apartment blocks and buildings alongside ancient temples, tombs and shrines.

The temple at Luxor was built to honour Amun, king of the gods, and the city gradually grew around it until it became Thebes, capital of the ancient Egyptian empire.

Luxor

On the West Bank lies the famous Valley of the Kings, the burial place for pharaohs from the 18th, 19th and 20th dynasties, including the tomb of Tutankhamun, who reigned between around 1336 and 1327 BCE. His tomb is world-famous because it was the most complete tomb ever found when it was discovered, and contained over 5,000 precious objects.

the Valley of the Kings

Menna was an important **scribe** and overseer of the pharaoh's fields. The hunting scene below was painted in his tomb around 1400 and 1352 BCE, and shows Menna and his family and an abundance of wildlife in papyrus marshes on the Nile. He is shown twice in the same image. On the left, he holds a **decoy bird** and throw stick, and on the right, he catches a tilapia fish, a symbol of **regeneration**.

GIZA

The city of Giza, the third-largest city in Egypt, contains possibly the most recognised of all Egyptian landmarks. Here, on the West Bank of the Nile, are the three famous pyramids and a giant sphinx.

A pyramid is a necropolis, or elaborate tomb, for a pharaoh. The sphinx was thought to have the head of Khafre, the pharaoh who was buried in the largest pyramid, and the body of a lion. It's carved directly from the sandstone in which it sits.

The Great Pyramid, the largest of the group, was built around 2600 BCE as the tomb of pharaoh Khufu. It was built from sandstone and covered in gleaming white limestone. Blocks of granite from Aswan were used inside the "King's Chamber" in the pyramid.

These materials would have been transported on the Nile. For a long time, no one could understand how the ancient Egyptians had moved such huge, heavy rocks into place, but the recently discovered remains of an old branch of the Nile beneath the pyramids sheds light on this. They may have been brought right up to the building site, floating on the water.

The pyramids are famous examples of the extraordinary technical and engineering ability of ancient Egyptians. For more than 4,000 years the Great Pyramid was the tallest building in the world, at 147 metres.

BOATS OF THE NILE

The Nile has always been an important highway for transporting food, people and materials throughout Egypt and beyond, so boats have been vital to Egypt's life.

The journey from Luxor to Cairo would have taken up to 20 days by wooden boat.

Boatbuilders were so important in ancient Egypt that images on the walls of tombs even show details of boatbuilding.

Early papyrus boats

In ancient times, reeds from the papyrus plant were cut and tied together in bundles to form canoe-shaped boats powered by oars.

By 3000 BCE, larger, more complex, boats were made from Egyptian acacia (a hard wood) and cedar wood from Lebanon, and were tied together with rope made from flax and grasses. These ropes were so strong and long-lasting that one made 4,600 years ago has even survived to this day. These boats were powered by sails, oars and sometimes both. They even had a steering system.

Some old boat designs can still be seen in modern boats on the Nile today. Felucca are small wind-powered boats often used for fishing. Dahabiya are similar to felucca boats, but with cabins and indoor space so they can be used for longer journeys.

Today, many boats use motors. Large ferry boats carry people along the river, and cruise ships – some with swimming pools – carry tourists.

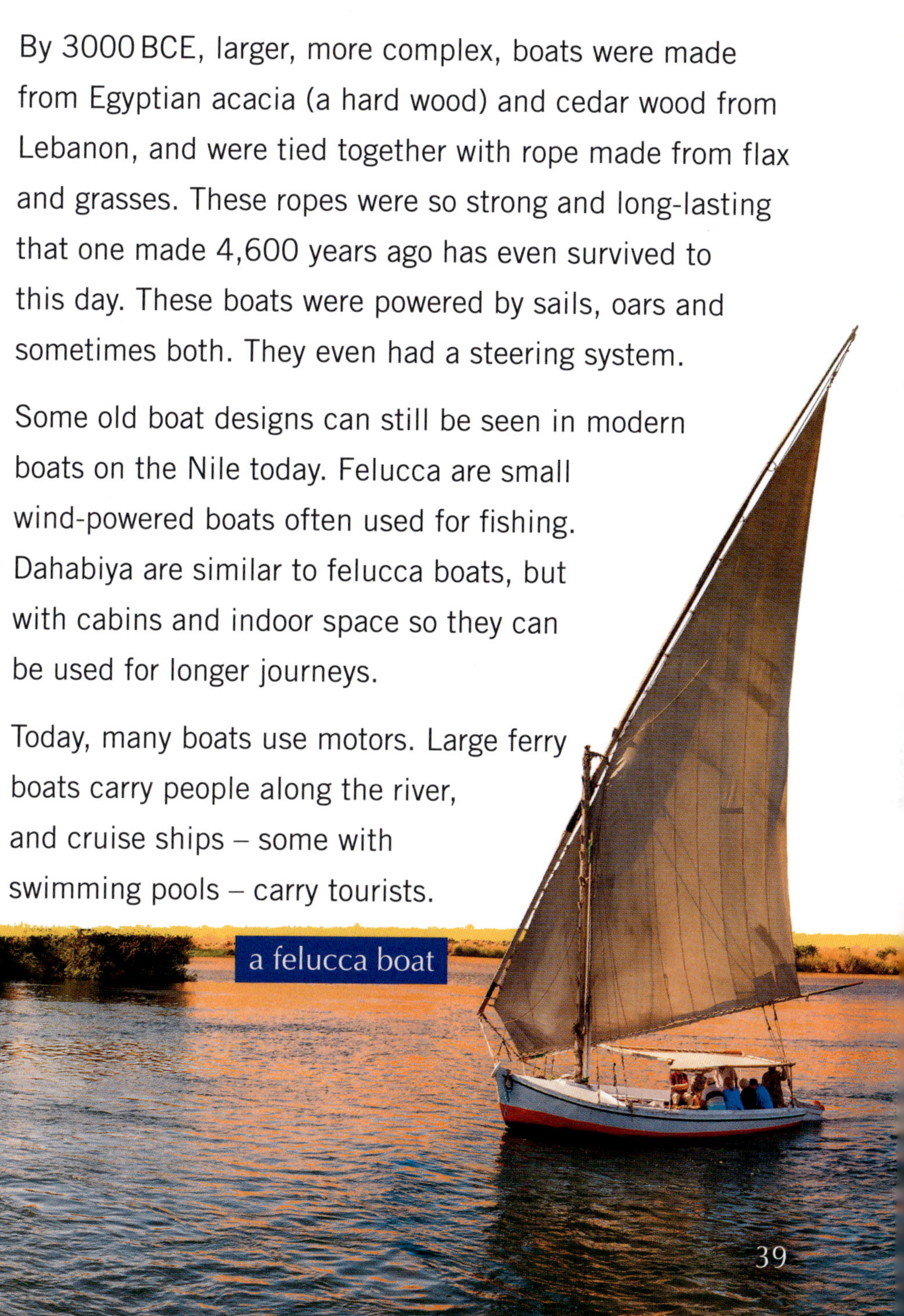
a felucca boat

Solar boats

Egyptians believed that the god of the sun, Ra, travelled through the sky on a barge boat, providing daylight to the world each day. Sunset meant that he and his vessel had travelled over the horizon to the underworld where, every night, he would have to defeat the enormous serpent Apophis before he could leave the underworld and travel through the sky again.

Some pharaohs were believed to be a representation of the sun god Ra on Earth and were given solar barges for their funerals or buried with boats alongside their pyramids to help them travel to the afterlife.

The most famous of these boats is the Khufu ship. It was found almost by accident while experts were cleaning the pyramids at Giza.

The boat was found in 1,200 pieces, and it took 14 years for Ahmed Youssef Moustafa, an Egyptian restorer, to put it back together. Thanks to his hard work, we can see how it would have looked around 2500 BCE when it was built for Pharaoh Khufu.

3 CAIRO AND THE NILE DELTA

Mediterranean Sea
Alexandria
NILE DELTA
Cairo

CAIRO

Egypt's capital city and its largest, is Cairo and is home to more than ten million people. Skyscrapers and modern buildings crowd alongside older buildings. Thousands of years ago this large city started out as a place of settlements and forts, placed next to the Nile. Here, the river leaves the Nile Valley and enters the **Delta**.

Over many years, the Nile's path has altered because all rivers naturally move and change. Much of the land on which modern-day Cairo stands has, in the past, been underwater – the city is actually built on sand dunes and old riverbanks.

Ancient Egyptian gods

Ra, the sun god, ruled all parts of the world, especially the sun, the sky, the pharaohs and order. He was the giver of life, warmth and growth and was considered King of the Gods.

Ra's place of worship in ancient Egyptian times was in Heliopolis, now part of Cairo.

THE NILE DELTA

Downriver from Cairo, as we approach the sea, the land surrounding the river changes from hills into large, flat plains, and the water slows down; this area is known as the Delta.

In ancient times, this area was known as Lower Egypt. The river divides into two: the wider Rosetta branch and the narrower Damietta branch. Both branches take the Nile for roughly 160 kilometres to the Mediterranean Sea.

As the water spreads out, the river slows and any silt it carries falls to the riverbed. Over many thousands of years, that silt has built up, creating land where there used to be sea.

Just as the silt provides fertile soil further up the Nile, it does the same here. The silt can be up to 20 metres deep, and creates rich soil for growing plants, so this is a very green area with lots of agriculture.

Mediterranean Sea

Damietta

Rashīd

Port Said

Alexandria

Damietta

Damanhūr

Ţanţā

Ismailia

Rosetta

Cairo

Giza

Nile

How does the Aswan Dam affect the Nile Delta?

Many are concerned that the construction of the Aswan Dam, even though it's hundreds of miles upstream, has led to big changes in the Nile Delta.

The Delta used to flood annually, spreading water and silt, but since the construction of the Aswan Dam that no longer happens. The dam also traps silt that would have ended up in the Delta, and the loss of its constant supply means that the coast is now **eroding**.

The fish, who feed on the nutrient-rich silt, have less to eat and freshwater lakes by the sea are turning saltier, so there's less fresh water.

The Delta floodplain

The large Delta **floodplain** is 250 kilometres wide. At the border with the sea, it turns into lagoons, salt marshes and lakes. Lake Mariut (also called Buhayrat Maryut) is the largest of the lakes, and historically an important port and trading place.

Underwater archaeology

In the last 30 years underwater **archaeologist** Franck Goddio and his team have discovered the remains of two lost cities under the Delta's water. These cities were important ports for trade with Greece, but by the 8th century they had sunk beneath the water. Archaeological divers uncovered structures of buildings and hundreds of boats and raised many valuable historical discoveries to the surface, including bronze incense burners, gold jewellery and a huge statue of a king, which would have greeted Greek sailors approaching the mouth of the Nile from the sea.

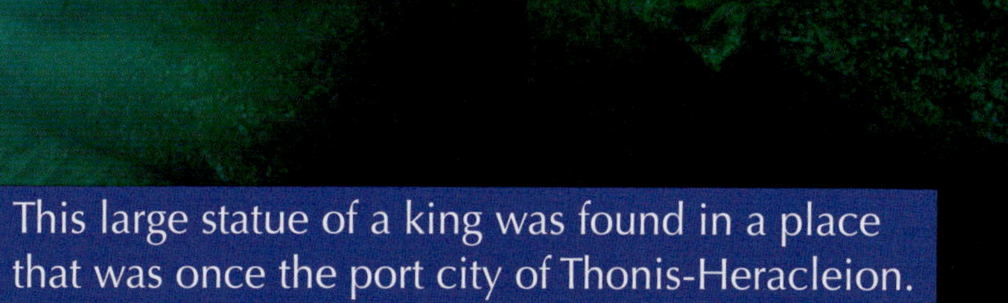

This large statue of a king was found in a place that was once the port city of Thonis-Heracleion.

A vital wetland for animals and birds

Hippos and Nile crocodiles that once lived in the Nile are now extinct in the Delta, but many other animals can still be found in the waters.

Nile monitor lizard

green turtle

Egyptian tortoise

loggerhead turtle

The Nile area is an important part of the route for millions of birds during migration, when they fly huge distances to get to and from their winter and summer homes. The wetland areas of the Nile Delta are a bit like service stations on a motorway – a vital point for birds to stop, rest for a while and feed.

Threats to the Delta

Climate warming is causing the levels in the Mediterranean Sea to rise, putting the Nile Delta in danger.

The current estimates say the sea is rising by 1.6 millimetres a year, causing saltwater to enter freshwater zones and threaten wildlife and plants. Around 15% of Egypt's best farmland has already been damaged.

The Delta's green land is also threatened as Egypt's cities continue to grow quickly.

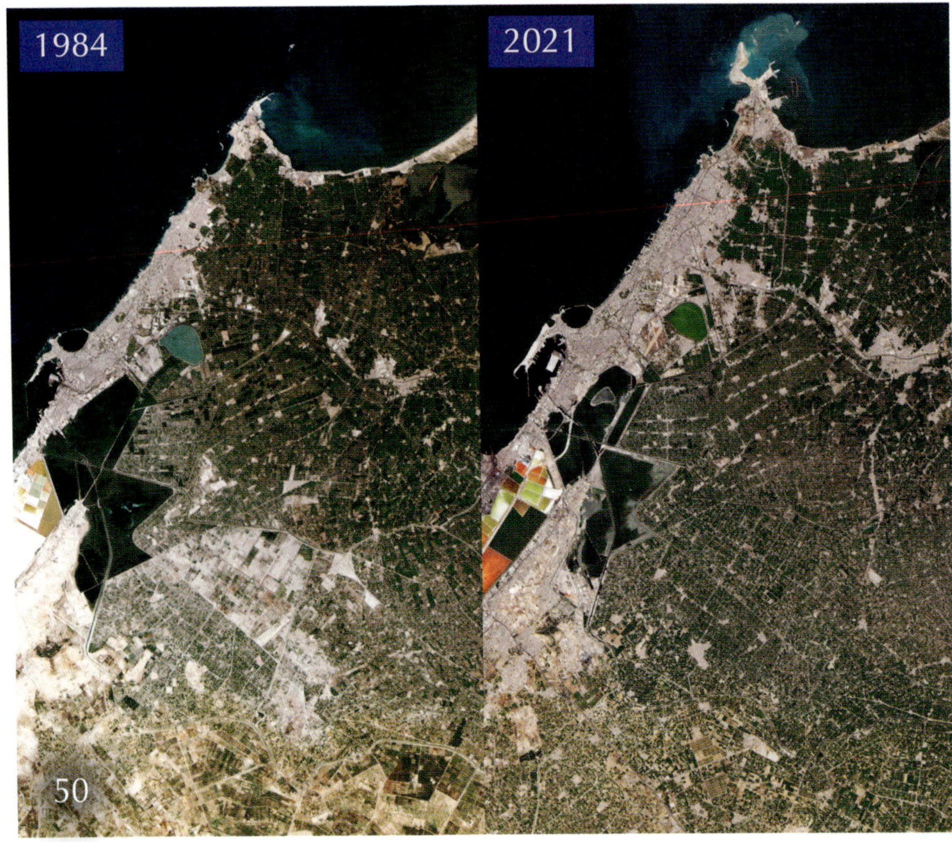

ALEXANDRIA

We end our Nile journey at Alexandria, the largest city on the Mediterranean coast. It was named after the Macedonian King Alexander the Great, who founded it in 331 BCE, despite only staying for a few months. In the reign of the pharaohs, it was the capital city of Egypt.

The Nile has always been critical to bringing life to Egypt's desert. All aspects of human life depend on it, from water to food, travel to building, and without it we wouldn't have the precious history or present-day Egypt. The constant presence of the Nile has created a land where old still meets new.

Here, after around 6,650 kilometres, the Nile river finally joins the Mediterranean Sea.

GLOSSARY

archaeologist someone who studies human history by digging up remains and objects

decoy bird a real or fake bird used to attract birds to within hunting range

delta a wetland that forms when a river slows down and drops silt as it enters the sea

eroding the wearing down and removal of rock by weather like wind and rain or water like rivers or glaciers

floodplain a broad, flat river valley at the lower end of a river

hieroglyphs a system of writing in pictures

mummified when a body was preserved by being rubbed with special oils and wrapped in cloth

pharaoh a ruler of ancient Egypt

rapid a fast-flowing and turbulent patch of river

regeneration various strategies to restore profitability and/or repopulate areas of the city deemed to be in decline

sand spits narrow banks of sand created by a river bend

scribe someone responsible for writing and keeping records

silt tiny particles of soil, sand or rock carried by a river

INDEX

Mediterranean Sea

THE NILE

Alexandria

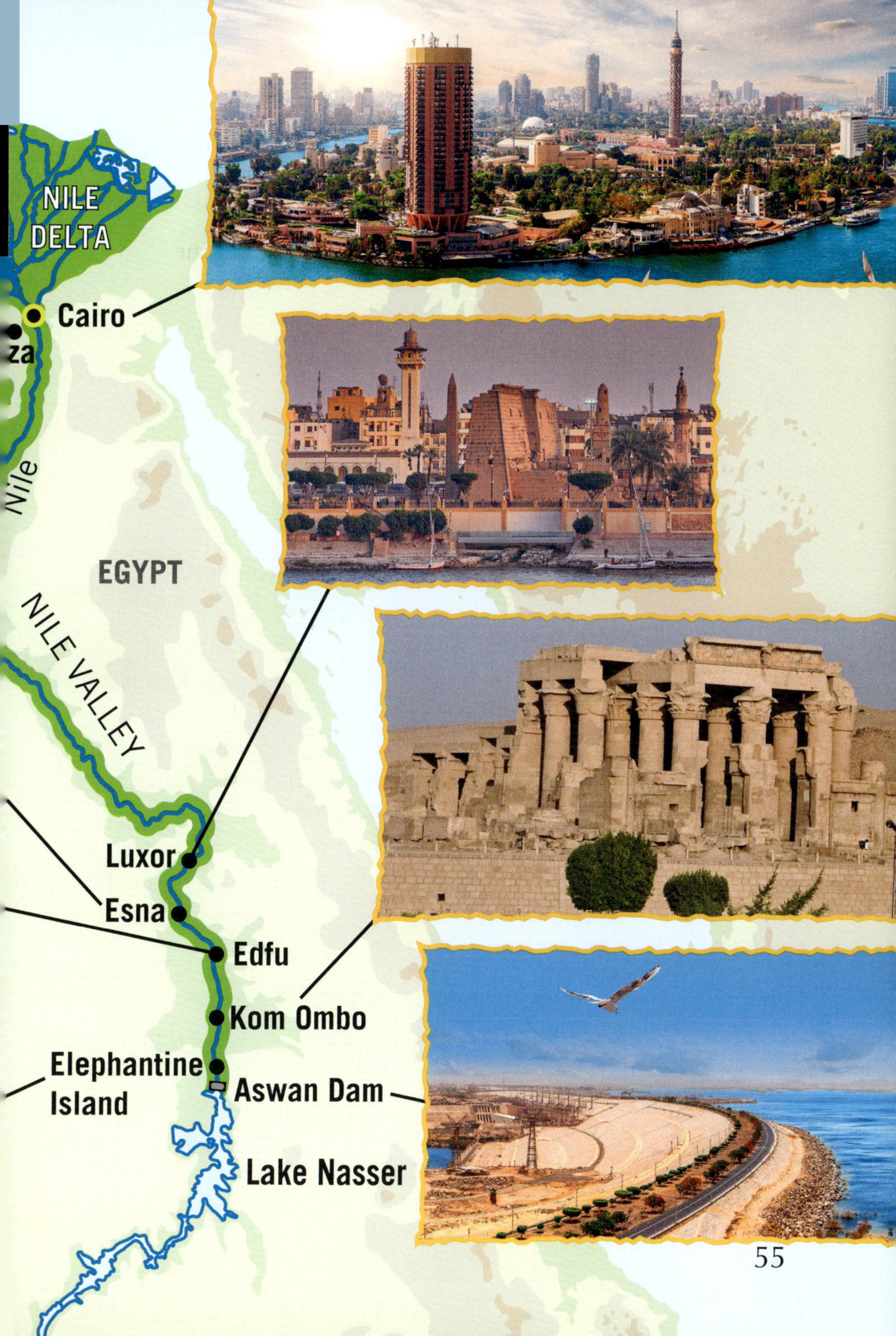
NILE
DELTA
Cairo
za
Nile
EGYPT
NILE VALLEY
Luxor
Esna
Edfu
Kom Ombo
Elephantine
Island
Aswan Dam
Lake Nasser

Which way is up?

Contents

Written by Emma Young

Collins

Over to you

In a moment, I'd like you to do something with this book. I want you to close it, lift it up high with both hands, hold it flat and let go. (But not over a rubbish bin. Or a puddle. A desk or a bed would be ideal!) Then I'd like you to pick it up and open it again to this page.

OK, you can do it now …

What happened?

If the book dropped, that might not be a *huge* surprise. But it's very good news. It means that gravity did its thing.

What *is* gravity?

Gravity is a force.

A force pushes on or pulls at an object. This can affect how the object moves.

When you shove a door shut, you use a push force to move that door *away* from you.

Gravity is a pull force. This means that other things are *pulled towards* whatever's making that gravity.

Every object in the universe has gravity. So that includes you, a car, a sheep and even a pea!

But the more **massive** the object, the greater its gravity.

Planet Earth is *so* massive that its gravity totally overwhelms yours. Earth's gravity is the reason you don't float off into space. It also keeps water in the oceans, cars on roads, sheep in fields and peas on your plate.

One way to picture it is to imagine an elastic band stretching from the middle of Earth, all the way out to you. If you jump up, it pulls you back down.

What else does gravity do?

Here are some brilliant reasons to be glad that gravity exists.

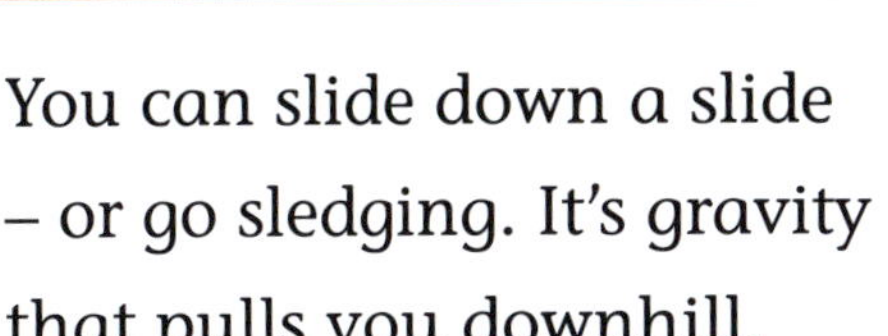

You can slide down a slide – or go sledging. It's gravity that pulls you downhill.

You can bounce up and down on a trampoline. Without gravity, one bounce up and you'd be off!

You can play football.

You don't have to strap yourself into bed at night. Or strap your bed to the floor!

Gravity can be tricky to think about because you can't see it. But it has huge effects on you and everything around you.

Sensing gravity

Are you ready to try something else?

In a moment, I'd like you to close your eyes. Then gently roll your head towards one shoulder. With your eyes still closed, I'd like you to point up, towards the ceiling …

Did you manage it? If so, one of the reasons is that you can *sense* the pull of gravity.

Deep inside your ears are tiny bag-like **organs**. They're lined with **hair cells.** They also contain tiny, white crystals of a substance called calcium carbonate in a slimy gel.

When your head is upright, gravity makes those crystals settle at the bottom and press on some of the hairs – and the cells send this message to your brain.

If you tilt your head to the side, gravity makes the crystals move. Now they bend different hairs. Your brain uses all these messages to work out where "up" is.

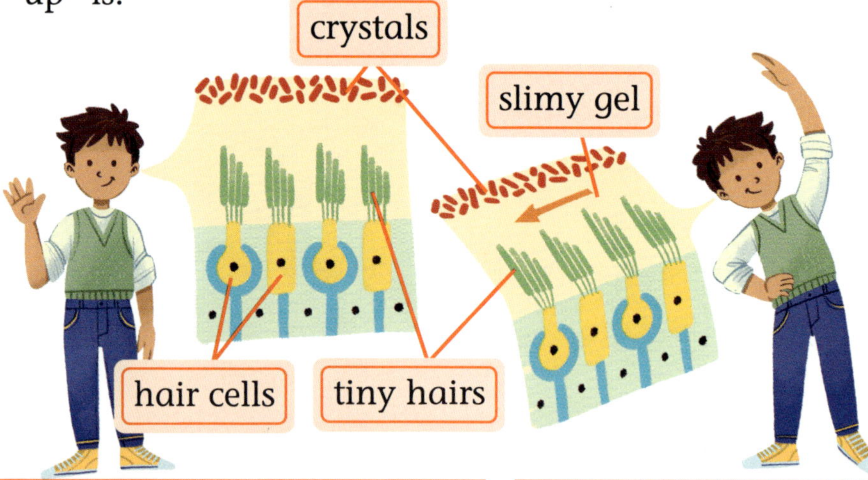

This is a close-up of an organ inside your ear when you are standing upright …

… and when you are leaning over.

Your brain uses your sense of gravity to help you to keep your balance.

A super sense

Have you ever wondered how a tree "knows" to grow *up* to the sky? Or how eyeless jellyfish "know" when they are swimming *up* towards the surface – or when they are drifting *down*?

In fact, other animals – and even plants – sense gravity, too.

Plants have cells that contain little **granules**. Earth's gravity makes those granules settle in the bottom of these cells. This tells plants where "up" is.

A jellyfish has an organ for sensing *gravity* that contains crystals and hair cells. It's very much like yours!

Your body in gravity

Your body **evolved** to exist in Earth's gravity.

Veins in your legs have flaps that help to keep blood flowing back towards your heart (rather than it all settling in your feet).

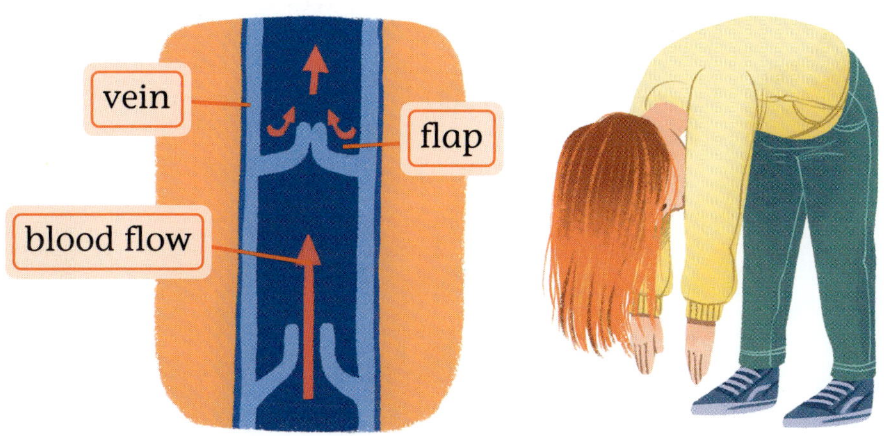

Mucus, aka snot, drips down and out of your nose. Without Earth's gravity, it would smother the cells that you need for smelling.

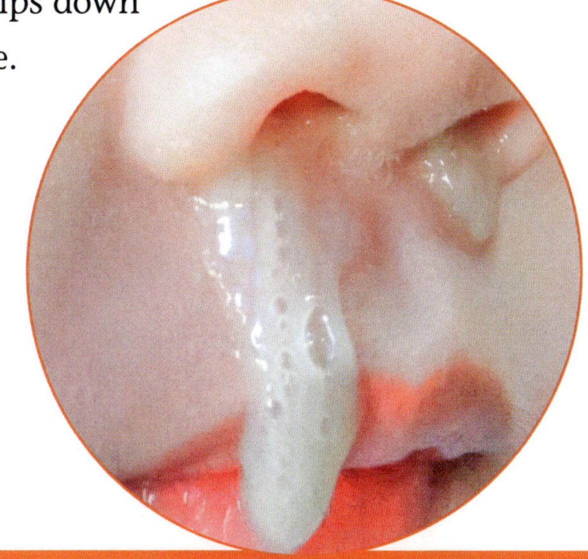

Fact!

You have lots of strong muscles that support your body *against* the downwards pull of Earth's gravity. Without those muscles, you'd collapse in a heap on the ground.

Weird weight

Are there any weighing scales around? If so, can you go and stand on them, to see what you weigh?

Now, if you could take those scales in a spaceship to the moon, do you think you'd weigh the same there?

You wouldn't.

Why not?

The amount of stuff in your body – your mass – would be the same.

But the moon is much smaller than Earth and has a lot *less mass* than our planet.

This means it has less gravity. So, on the moon, there'd be less of a pull on you – so you wouldn't press down as hard on the scales.

Fact!

You'd weigh *six times less* on the moon!

Earth is not all

The further away you get from an object, the less its gravity pulls on you. But there are objects that are *so* massive that even though they're a long way away, their gravity still affects us.

Have you ever been to the beach and noticed that sometimes the water comes really far up, but at other times, it shrinks right back?

This is a "high" tide.

This is a "low" tide.

These changes happen as the moon moves around, or "orbits", Earth. The moon is kept in place by Earth's gravity. But the *moon's* gravity pulls on the water in our seas and oceans!

The sun's gravity keeps all the planets in our solar system moving around it.

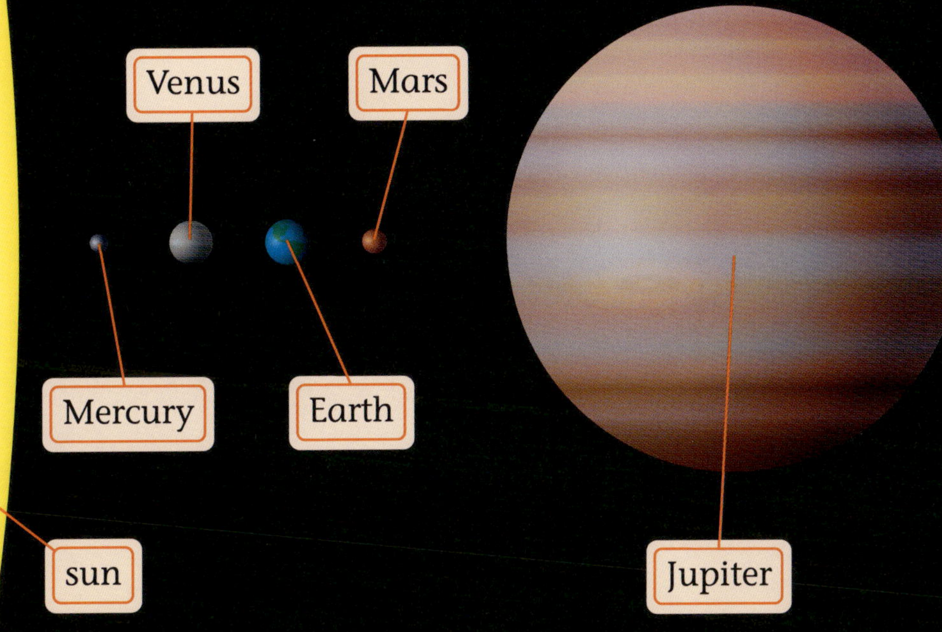

If the sun didn't have any gravity, Mars would go floating off in one direction – and we'd drift off in another!

Other planets have their own moons, all kept in place by their gravity.

Fact!

Jupiter has 95 moons. Imagine looking up at that busy sky!

Other orbits

The moon is what's called a natural satellite. Satellite is the word we use for any object that *moves around* another object.

But there are also about 8,400 human-made satellites whizzing around Earth! They, too, are kept in orbit by Earth's gravity.

Fact!
Though lots of these satellites don't work any more, they are still spinning around us.

These satellites do all sorts of things!

Some allow scientists to get a better look at amazing objects in space.

The Solar Orbiter satellite takes pictures of the sun.

Others enable navigation apps that can tell you where you are in the world. And when you're going the wrong way!

Blast off!

When astronauts go into space, they feel a *lot* less gravity than we feel on Earth. Scientists call it microgravity.

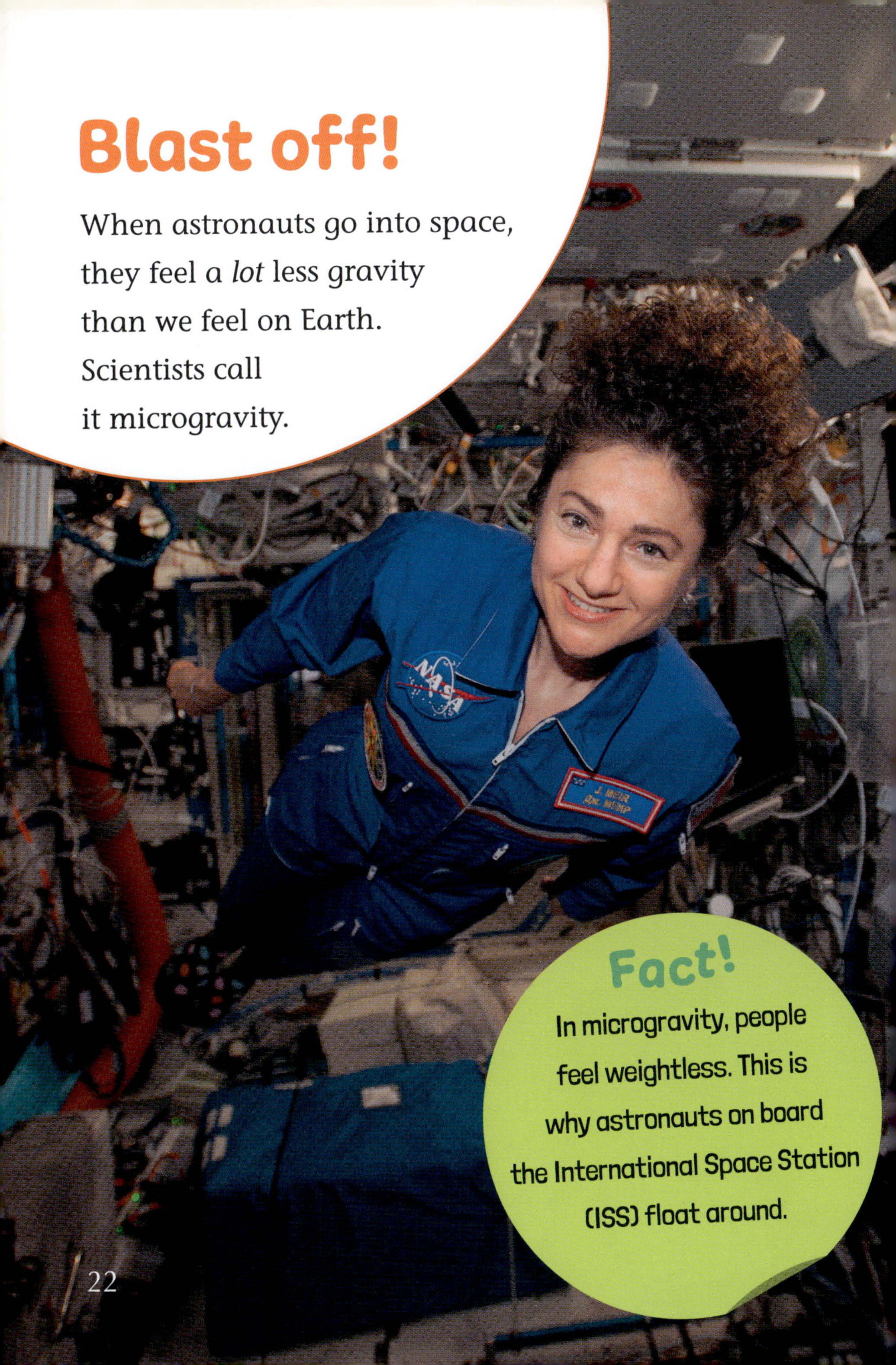

Fact!

In microgravity, people feel weightless. This is why astronauts on board the International Space Station (ISS) float around.

To live in microgravity, astronauts do all sorts of things differently.

They eat food straight from plastic packs or cans.

Bread isn't allowed on the International Space Station because the crumbs would float everywhere!

When they go to the toilet, they use a funnel to gather urine.

Without gravity, water isn't pulled downwards. This means astronauts can't have showers. They use wet towels and waterless shampoo instead.

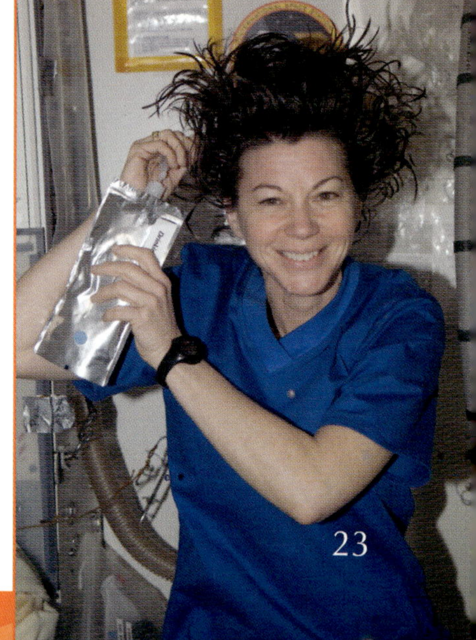

About half of all astronauts suffer from "space sickness" while they adjust to microgravity. Fortunately, there are specially designed bags to catch the vomit!

In the longer term, astronauts' bodies can suffer in other ways.

Muscles that they normally need to move around don't work so hard, so they start to waste away.

Bones, which are used to supporting their weight, get weaker, and shrink.

Scientists have spent a *lot* of time working out ways to help.

Astronauts on the ISS strap themselves into exercise equipment and work out for two hours every day. This helps to protect their muscles and bones.

A life force

Gravity rules our lives.

It keeps Earth moving around the sun.

It keeps the moon – and all the other satellites – in place around Earth.

It also keeps our feet on the ground (most of the time!)

It means we can play sports, run around, sit at a table and sleep safely at night – without fear of floating up and hitting our head on the ceiling.

And, if you let go of a book, you can be sure it'll drop to the ground.

Not bad for something that we can't even see!

Glossary

evolved developed gradually over a long time

granules particles of something

hair cells cells with hairs that stick out of them; when those hairs are bent, the cells send a message to the brain

massive an object that contains a lot of stuff

mucus slippery stuff inside your nose (and in other parts of your body) which protects the cells underneath and stops them from drying out

organs parts of the body with their own special jobs

veins tubes that carry "used" blood back to your heart

Index

Gravity ...

... is a pull force.

... is something we can sense.

... depends on the mass of the object creating it.

... keeps us, animals, and even the seas, down on the surface of Earth.

... keeps the moon and other satellites circling Earth.

... helps to explain our weight.

... rules the world!

Ideas for reading

Written by Gill Matthews
Primary Literacy Consultant

Reading objectives:

- discuss and clarify the meanings of words, linking new meanings to known vocabulary
- draw on what they already know or on background information and vocabulary provided by the teacher
- check that the text makes sense to them as they read and correcting inaccurate reading
- answer and ask questions

Spoken language objectives:

- ask relevant questions to extend their understanding and knowledge
- use relevant strategies to build their vocabulary
- articulate and justify answers, arguments and opinions

Curriculum links: Science: animals, including humans

Word count: 1514

Interest words: totally, gently, differently, fortunately, specially, normally, safely

Build a context for reading

- Ask children to look closely at the front cover and to read the title. Ask what the title means to them.
- Read the back-cover blurb. Ask for ideas for what the invisible force might be.
- Point out that this is an information book. Explore children's experience and knowledge of non-fiction and the typical features found in those books.
- Ask children to turn to the contents page. Discuss the purpose and organisation of a contents page.
- Ask children to use the contents to find the chapter called *Over to you*.

Ideas for reading

Written by Gill Matthews
Primary Literacy Consultant

Reading objectives:

- check that the book makes sense to them, discussing their understanding and exploring the meaning of words in context
- distinguish between statements of fact and opinion
- retrieve, record and present information from non-fiction

Spoken language objectives:

- use relevant strategies to build their vocabulary
- participate in discussions, presentations, performances, role play, improvisations and debates

Curriculum links: History: the achievements of the earliest civilisations

Interest words: mighty, fertile, harsh, advanced, rich, vital

Build a context for reading

- Ask children to look closely at the front cover of the book and to read the title. Discuss what they can see on the cover.
- Read the back-cover blurb. Explore children's knowledge of the Nile river and Egypt. Discuss what they expect to find out from the book.
- Point out that this is an information book. Ask children to tell you as much as they can about non-fiction texts, their typical features, layout, purpose etc.
- Give them a few minutes to skim the book and to identify which features this book contains.

Understand and apply reading strategies

- Read pp2–3 aloud, asking children to follow the route described on the map on p3.
- Read pp4-5 together and point out the phrase *he was said to have*. Compare it to the opening sentence on p2. Establish that one is an opinion and one is a fact. Discuss why it is important to be able to differentiate between the two.